How to ⌇⌇⌇⌇ ⌇

to Christ

THROUGH SIMPLE QUESTIONS

By Jesse Ellison

Charleston, AR:
COBB PUBLISHING
2018

Published in the United States of America by:

Cobb Publishing
704 E. Main St.
Charleston, AR 72933
CobbPublishing.com
CobbPublishing@gmail.com
(479) 747-8372

The questions you are about to read on the next page were answered through science hundreds of years ago, but as you will discover, the Bible answered them long before science ever could. Ask yourself, 'How is this possible?' Simply stated, the Bible is the truth.

Can you prove there is a God using only the Bible?

Consider the following questions:

- How did Abram know to circumcise on the eighth day when science did not discover the truth behind the vitamin K levels to prevent death until recent centuries?

- How did Job know the stars sing to each other (Job 38:7)? Science just recently found this to be true.

- What about fresh water springs in the ocean (Job 38:16)? The springs were officially discovered by man in the 1900s.

- Isaiah 40:22 says the earth is a circle, but, as a society, we were taught in school Christopher Columbus made that discovery.

- Jeremiah wrote about gravitational pull (Jeremiah 31:35), whereas science discovered the gravitational pull from Isaac Newton (a strong believer in God and the Bible), and later made the connection between gravitational pull and the tides of the ocean.

- Job 26:7 says the earth sets on nothing. How did Job know this?

Dear Friend,

I know that you have a love and appreciation for God, and that you want to spend eternity in His presence with Jesus Christ.

That is why I know you will want to go through this brief set of Bible questions—you want to *know* without a doubt that you are saved, and you want to know *how* to bring others to that same level of knowledge and confidence.

These questions are all answered straight from the Bible, and we've even provided you the verses that answer them.

All you have to do is read the question, write down your answer, and then turn the page to see if your answer matches with what God's Word says. It's very simple, but also very powerful.

By the time you finish this extremely short booklet (if you take the time to consider the verses), you will know more about God's Word and salvation than over 99% of the world!

So, go ahead and turn the page and get started. ***But remember one thing***: If God said it, it must be true, regardless of what any well-meaning religious people may say or teach.

Okay, let's get to it!

The first question is an easy one, and something you'll want to answer so that you have something to compare with the Bible later on in this study.

How were you saved?

1. Do God, Christ, and the Holy Spirit disagree on how someone is saved?

For there are three that bear record in heaven, **_the Father, the Word, and the Holy Ghost: and_** **_these three are one_**. *And there are three that bear witness in earth, the Spirit, and the water, and the blood: and these three agree in one (1 John 5:7-8).*

2. Does God want his children to all believe the same way?

*Now I beseech you, brethren, by the name of our Lord Jesus Christ, that **ye all speak the same thing**, and that there be no divisions among you; but that ye be perfectly joined together in the same mind and in the same judgment (1 Corinthians 1:10).*

3. Do you think all faiths are right?

*There is... One Lord, **<u>one faith</u>**, one baptism (Ephesians 4:4-5)*

4. How does someone know their faith is right?

*So then faith cometh by hearing, and **_hearing by the word of God_** (Romans 10:17).*

5. Can someone know God without hearing the gospel?

*How then shall they call on him in whom they have not believed? and **how shall they believe in him of whom they have not heard?** and how shall they hear without a preacher? (Romans 10:14)*

6. How did you find out about Grace and Truth?

*And the **Word was made flesh**, and dwelt among us (and we beheld his glory, the glory as of the only begotten of the Father), **full of grace and truth** (John 1:14).*

7. Should I prove myself to God?

Study to show thyself approved unto God, a workman that needeth not to be ashamed, rightly dividing the word of truth (2 Timothy 2:15).

8. What is your definition of believe?

*He that **believeth** on the Son hath everlasting life:
and he that **believeth** not the Son shall not see
life; but the wrath of God abideth on him (John
3:36).*

Though these words appear to be the same in
English, they are actually quite different in the
original Greek language.

The first word translated "believeth" in this
verse is defined by the experts as "trust."

The second time "believeth" appears in this
verse, it is a different Greek word which means
"obey."

9. Is your belief any different than the devils?

*Thou believest that there is one God, thou doest well: **the devils also believe**, and tremble (James 2:19).*

10. Has God given you everything you need to know in the Bible?

*All scripture is given by inspiration of God, and is profitable for doctrine, for reproof, for correction, for instruction in righteousness: that the man of God may be perfect, throughly furnished unto **all good works*** (2 Timothy 3:16-17).

---

*His divine power has given to us **all things that pertain unto life and godliness*** (2 Peter 1:3).

11. Does God want you to study the Bible?

__Study to show thyself approved__ unto God, a workman that needeth not to be ashamed, rightly dividing the word of truth (Timothy 2:15).

12. Is it important to study the Bible?

*These were more noble than those in Thessalonica, in that they received the word with all readiness of mind and **searched the scriptures daily**, whether those things were so (Acts 17:11).*

13. Does God want you to teach?

__Teaching__ them to observe all things whatsoever I have commanded __you__; and, lo, I am with you alway, even unto the end of the world. Amen (Matthew 28:20).

For when for the time __ye ought to be teachers__, ye have need that one teach you again which be the first principles of the oracles of God; and are become such as have need of milk, and not of strong meat (Hebrews 5:12).

14. How does someone find the truth?

*Sanctify them through thy truth; thy **word** is truth (John 17:17).*

15. Could you be a false teacher and not realize it?

*And with all deceivableness of unrighteousness in them that perish; because they received not the love of the truth that they might be saved. And for this cause God shall send them **strong delusion**, that **they should believe a lie**; That they all might be damned who believed not the truth, but had pleasure in unrighteousness (2 Thessalonians 2:10-12).*

16. What should we do if we hear false teaching?

*Now I beseech you, brethren, mark them which cause divisions and offences contrary to the doctrine which ye have learned; and **avoid them** (Romans 16:17).*

17. Do you believe more people are going to hell or heaven?

*Enter ye in at the straight gate; for wide is the gate, and broad is the way, that leadeth to destruction and **many** there be which go in thereat: Because straight is the gate, and narrow is the way which leadeth unto life and **few** there be that find it (Matthew 7:13-14).*

18. Do you believe the devil wants people to depend on their feelings and opinions?

*Not every one that saith unto me, Lord, Lord, shall enter into the kingdom of heaven; but he that doeth the will of my Father which is in heaven. Many will say to me in that day, Lord, Lord, have we not prophesied in thy name? and in thy name have cast out devils? And in thy name done many wonderful works? And then will I profess unto them, **I never knew you**; depart from me, ye that work iniquity (Matthew 7:21-23).*

19. Are you supposed to judge?

*Judge not according to the appearance, but **judge righteous** judgment (John 7:24).*

20. Do you judge yourself?

*But let a man examine himself and so let him eat of that bread and drink of that cup... For if we would **<u>judge ourselves</u>** we should not be judged (1 Corinthians 11:28-31).*

21. How will you be judged?

And I saw the dead, small and great, stand before God; and the books were opened: and another book was opened, which is the book of life: and **_the dead were judged out of those things which were written in the books, according to their works_**. *And the sea gave up the dead which were in it; and death and hell delivered up the dead which were in them: and they were judged every man according to their works. And death and hell were cast into the lake of fire. This is the second death. And whosoever was not found written in the book of life was cast into the lake of fire (Revelation 20:12-15).*

22. Do we need to put our faith in action?

*But whoso looketh into the perfect law of liberty, and continueth therein, he being not a forgetful hearer, but a **doer** of the work, this man shall be blessed in his deed (James 1:25).*

23. What does repentance mean?

*But showed first unto them of Damascus, and at Jerusalem, and throughout all the coasts of Judaea, and then to the Gentiles, that they should repent and **turn to God**, and **do works meet for repentance**. (Acts 26:20).*

24. Why do you repent?

*Repent ye therefore and be converted that your **sins may be blotted out**, when the time of refreshing shall come from the presence of the Lord (Acts 3:19).*

25. Do we have to do something for God to hear us?

*Now we know that God heareth not sinners; but if any man be a worshiper of God, and **doeth his will**, him he heareth (John 9:31).*

26. Does God want us to love him? How do you show God you love him?

*If ye love me, **<u>keep</u>** my commandments (John 14:15).*

---

*Ye are my friends, if you **<u>do whatsoever I have commanded you</u>** (John 15:14).*

27. How do we abide in God's love?

*If **ye keep my commandments**, ye shall abide in my love, even as I have kept my Father's commandments and abide in his love (John 15:10).*

28. Does God expect us to do good works?

*For we are his workmanship, created in Christ Jesus unto good works, which God hath before ordained that we should **_walk in them_** (Ephesians 2:10).*

29. How does someone find Grace?

*For by grace are ye saved through **faith** and that not of yourselves. It is the gift of God (Ephesians 2:8).*

30. Do we have to obey God to have Grace?

*By whom we have received grace and apostleship for **obedience** to the faith among all nations, for his name (Romans 1:5).*

31. Can you lose your salvation?

*For I testify unto every man that heareth the words of the prophecy of this book, If any man shall add unto these things, God shall add unto him the plagues that are written in this book: And if any man shall take away from the words of the book of this prophecy, God shall **take away his part out of the book of life**, and out of the holy city, and from the things which are written in this book (Revelation 22:18-19).*

---

*Look to yourselves, **that we lose not those things which we have wrought**, but that we receive a full reward (2 John 8)*

32. Can a Christian fall from grace? (remember that it is impossible to fall from something if you were never there in the first place)

*Paul, an apostle, (not of men, neither by man, but by Jesus Christ, and God the Father, who raised him from the dead;) and all the brethren which are with me, **unto the churches of Galatia** (Galatians 1:1-2).*

*Christ is become of no effect unto you, whosoever of you are justified by the law; **ye are fallen from grace**. (Galatians 5:4)*

33. If someone fell from grace what should that person do?

Repent therefore of this thy wickedness, and pray God, if perhaps the thought of thine heart may be forgiven thee (Acts 8:22).

———————————————

If we confess our sins, he is faithful and just to forgive us our sins, and to cleanse us from all unrighteousness (1 John 1:9)

34. Who is covered by the blood of Jesus?

*Take heed therefore unto yourselves, and to all the flock of God, over the which the Holy Ghost hath made you overseers, to feed **the church of God, which he hath purchased with his own blood*** *(Acts 20:28).*

35. What does the word "church" mean?

The original Greek word translated "church" is ekklesia, which literally means "Called out."

36. How many true churches are there?

*And I say also unto thee, That thou art Peter, and upon this rock I will build **my church**; and the gates of hell shall not prevail against it (Matthew 16:18).*

37. Who is the head of your church?

For the husband is the head of the wife, even as **_Christ_** *is the head of the church and he is the savior of the body (Ephesians 5:23).*

38. Is the church and the body of Christ the same thing?

*And hath put all things under his feet and gave him to be the head over all things to **the church, which is his body**, the fullness of him that filleth all in all (Ephesians 1:23).*

39. How did you get into your church?

*For as the body is one, and hath many members, and all the members of that one body, being many, are one body: so also is Christ. For by one Spirit are we all **baptized into one body**, whether we be Jews or Gentiles, whether we be bond or free; and have been all made to drink into one Spirit (1 Corinthians 12:12-13).*

40. Who adds you to the church?

*Praising God and having favor with all the people. And the **Lord** added to the church daily such as should be saved (Acts 2:47).*

41. What is the Gospel?

*Moreover, brethren I declare unto you the gospel which I preached unto you, which also ye have received, and wherein ye stand; By which also ye are saved,if ye keep in memory what I preached unto you, unless ye have believed in vain. For I delivered unto you first of all that which I also received how that Christ **died** for our sins according to the scriptures; And that he was **buried**, and that he **rose again** the third day according to the scriptures (1 Corinthians 15:1-4).*

42. What happens if someone doesn't obey the Gospel?

In **_flaming fire_**, taking vengeance on them that know not God, and that obey not the Gospel of our Lord Jesus Christ (2 Thessalonians 1:8).

43. How do you obey the Gospel?

Know ye not, that so many of us as were baptized into Jesus Christ were baptized into his death? Therefore we are buried with him by baptism into death; that like as Christ was raised up from the dead by the glory of the Father, even so we also should walk in newness of life. For if we have been planted together in the likeness of his death, we shall be also in the likeness of his resurrection: Knowing this, that our old man is crucified with him, that the body of sin might be destroyed, that henceforth we should not serve sin. For he that is dead is freed from sin (Romans 6:3-7).

      Crucified—Romans 6:6
      Death—Romans 6:3
      Burial—Romans 6:4
      Resurrection—Romans 6:5
      Freed—Romans 6:7

44. Are you commanded to be baptized?

Go ye therefore, and teach all nations, *baptizing* them in the name of the Father, and of the Son, and of the Holy Ghost, Teaching them to observe all things whatsoever I have *commanded* you: and lo, I am with you alway, even unto the end of the world. Amen (Matthew 28:19-20).

———————————————

And he [Peter] *commanded them to be baptized* in the name of the Lord (Acts 10:48).

45. Is Christ the savior of the church?

*For the husband is the head of the wife, even as Christ is the head of the church and he is the **savior** of the body (Ephesians 5:23).*

46. Why were you baptized?

47. Do you need to understand why to be baptized?

*Then they that gladly **<u>received his word</u>** were baptized and the same day there were added unto them about three thousand souls (Acts 2:41).*

48. Were you saved before you were baptized?

*And with many other words did he testify and exhort, saying, **Save yourselves** from this untoward generation. Then **they that gladly received his word were baptized**: and the same day there were added unto them about three thousand souls... Praising God, and having favor with all the people. And the Lord added to the church daily such as should be saved (Acts 2:40-41, 47).*

49. Was John the Baptist baptizing for forgiveness of sins?

John did baptize in the wilderness, and preach the baptism of repentance for the remission of sins (Mark 1:4).

50. Was the thief on the cross baptized?

*And there went out unto him all the land of Judaea, and they of Jerusalem, and were **all** baptized of him [John the baptist] in the river of Jordan, confessing their sins (Mark 1:5).*

51. How many valid baptisms are there in the New Testament?

*There is... One Lord, one faith, **one** baptism (Ephesians 4:4-5).*

52. Does baptism require water?

*And as they went on their way, they came unto a certain water: and the eunuch said, See, **here is water; what doth hinder me to be baptized?** (Acts 8:36).*

53. Does baptism mean buried?

Buried *with him in baptism, wherein also ye are risen with him through the faith of the operation of God, who hath raised him from the dead (Colossians 2:12).*

54. How is God involved in baptism?

*In whom also ye are circumcised with **the circumcision made without hands**, in putting off the body of the sins of the flesh by the circumcision of Christ: Buried with him in baptism, wherein also ye are risen with him though the faith of the **operation of God**, who hath raised him from the dead (Colossians 2:11-12).*

55. What must you do to be in Christ?

*For as many of you as have been **<u>baptized into Christ</u>** have put on Christ (Galatians 3:27).*

56. How does someone receive heavenly blessings?

*Blessed be the God and Father of our Lord Jesus Christ, who hath blessed us with all spiritual blessings in heavenly places **in Christ** (Ephesians 1:3).*

57. Can someone go to heaven by just being a good person?

*If a man **abide not in me** [Christ], he is cast forth as a branch, and is withered and men gather them and cast them into the fire, and they are burned (John 15:6).*

58. What do you seek in life?

But seek ye first the kingdom of God, and his righteousness, and all these things shall be added unto you. Take therefore no thought for the morrow, for the morrow shall take thought for the things of itself. Sufficient unto the day is the evil thereof (Matthew 6:33-34).

59. Who do you put first in your life?

*And thou shalt **love the Lord thy God** with all thy heart, and with all thy soul, and with all thy mind, and with all thy strength: this is the first commandment (Mark 12:30).*

60. Are you helping people get to heaven?

__Let your light shine__ before men, that they may see your good works and glorify your Father which is in heaven (Matthew 5:16).

61. Do you try to live like Christ?

*When Christ, **who is our life**, shall appear, then shall ye also will appear with him in Glory (Colossians 3:4).*

62. Is it important to stay away from certain people?

*Be not deceived; evil communications **corrupt** good manners (1 Corinthians 15:33).*

63. Does God want us to stay away from those who corrupt people?

___**Abstain**___ *from all appearance of evil*
(1 Thessalonians 5:22).

Why?

Evil Pursueth sinners: but to the righteous good
shall be repayed.

64. Why is it important for us to worship God?

*Not forsaking the assembling of ourselves together, as the manner of some is, but exhorting one another, and so much the more as ye see the day approaching. For if we sin willfully after that we have received the knowledge of the truth, there remaineth **no more sacrifice for sins** (Hebrews 10:25-26).*

65. Who wrote more books of the New Testament than anyone else?

Saul of Tarsus, who was also known as the apostle Paul (this can be seen in Acts 13, as well as the first few verses of every book from Romans to Philemon)

66. What did he have to do to have his sins forgiven?

*And now why tarriest thou? Arise and be **baptized** and wash away thy sins, calling on the name of the Lord (Acts 22:16).*

67. Who decides when you're baptized?

*And as they went on their way, they came unto a certain water and **the eunuch said, See, here is water. What doth hinder me to be baptized?** And Phillip said, If thou believest with all thine heart thou mayest. And he answered and said, I believe that Jesus Christ is the Son of God. And he commanded the chariot to stand still; and they went down both into the water, both Phillip and the eunuch; and he baptized him (Acts 8:36-38).*

68. Who adds you to the church?

*Praising God and having favor with all the people. And the **Lord** added to the church daily such as should be saved (Acts 2:47).*

69. How frequently did baptisms occur?

*Praising God, and having favor with all the people. And the Lord added to the church **daily** such as should be saved (Acts 2:47).*

70. Should we wait until baptisms are scheduled?

*And they spake unto him the word of the Lord, and to all that were in his house. And he took them **_the same hour of the night_**, and washed their stripes; and **_was baptized_**, he and all his, **_straightway_** (Acts 16:32-33).*

71. Does your baptism have to match with Bible baptism in order to be valid to God?

72. Were you baptized *after* you believed?

Then ***they that gladly received his word were baptized***: and the same day there were added unto them about three thousand souls. (Acts 2:41)

73. Were you baptized *after* you repented?

*Then Peter said unto them, **Repent, and be baptized** every one of you in the name of Jesus Christ for the remission of sins, and ye shall receive the gift of the Holy Ghost. (Acts 2:38)*

74. Was your baptism for the remission of sins?

*Then Peter said unto them, Repent, and be baptized every one of you in the name of Jesus Christ **for the remission of sins**, and ye shall receive the gift of the Holy Ghost. (Acts 2:38)*

75. Were you baptized so your sins could be washed away, or were they already washed away before baptism?

*And now why tarriest thou? arise, and **be baptized, and wash away thy sins**, calling on the name of the Lord. (Acts 22:16)*

76. When you were baptized, was it to remove your sins, or were your sins already removed?

*In whom also ye are circumcised with the circumcision made without hands, in **putting off the body of the sins of the flesh** by the circumcision of Christ: Buried with him in baptism, wherein also ye are risen with him through the faith of the operation of God, who hath raised him from the dead. (Colossians 2:11-12)*

77. When you were baptized, was if *after* belief, but *before* salvation?

*He that believeth and is baptized **shall be saved**;*
he that believeth not shall be damned.
(Mark 16:16)

78. Did your baptism save you, or were you saved before baptism?

*The like figure whereunto even **baptism doth also now save us** (not the putting away of the filth of the flesh, but the answer of a good conscience toward God,) by the resurrection of Jesus Christ. (1 Peter 3:21)*

79. Did your baptism put you *into* Christ, or were you already *in* Christ?

*Know ye not, that so many of us as were **baptized into Jesus Christ** were baptized **into** his death? Therefore we are buried with him by baptism **into** death: that like as Christ was raised up from the dead by the glory of the Father, even so we also should walk in newness of life. (Romans 6:3-4)*

80. Was your baptism so important that you wanted it done immediately, or did you wait for days or weeks to get it done?

*And they spake unto him the word of the Lord, and to all that were in his house. And he took them **the same hour of the night**, and washed their stripes; and **was baptized**, he and all his, straightway. (Acts 16:32-33)*

81. If your baptism doesn't match with Bible baptism, should you be baptized properly, for the right reasons?

And he said unto them, Unto what then were ye baptized? And they said, Unto John's baptism. Then said Paul, John verily baptized with the baptism of repentance, saying unto the people, that they should believe on him which should come after him, that is, on Christ Jesus. ***When they heard this, they were baptized in the name of the Lord Jesus****. (Acts 19:3-5)*